Prayer Journal for Women

52 Week Christian Journal,
Devotional & Guided Bible Study for Women

Prayer Journal for Women

52 Week Christian Journal, Devotional & Guided Bible Study for Women

Abigail Miller

KALOGRIA PRESS

Note

Would you like to receive future books from Kalogria Press absolutely free?

Whenever we publish a new book we like to give away a dozen copies as a way of saying thank you to our readers.

If you enjoy this journal and would like the chance to receive one of our future giveaway copies then please email us your name and postal address to kalogriapress@gmail.com and we will enter you into the next draw.

NB. We will never share your personal details with anyone... ever.

Continue your journey with God at

www.kalogriapress.com

This journal belongs to....

....

Table of Contents

Welcome to your journey with God!

I'm so glad that you have made this wonderful choice to connect with God, and I know that the words and thoughts that you share in this journal will create a beautiful record to treasure.

As you'll see, this journal covers 12 whole months and gives you two pages for each of the 52 weeks. The weeks are not fixed to a particular date, so you can start this journal anytime you want. There is space at the top of the right-hand page of each week for you to write the current date if you wish.

At the beginning of each week, at the top of the left-hand page in a box, is your all-important weekly **_Scripture_**. Each Scripture sets a theme for the week and all 52 Scriptures have been collected into six different themes which are:

- Hope & Resilience
- Faith & Trust
- Love & Gratitude
- Perseverance & Patience
- Doubt & Fear
- Courage & Wisdom

Directly under the Scripture is a short commentary/study of the verse for you to consider, and under that are some questions and challenges designed to guide you on your journey and give you some ideas to work with.

And that beautiful floral illustration to the right of the Scripture on the left-hand page? Yes, as you reflect on the Scripture, please do color it in if you wish! Mindfulness is a great path to discovery.

My command is this :
Love each other as I have loved you.
~ John 15:12

Love Each Other

God's love for us is unconditional and boundless; it is through His love for us that He forgives our sins and reserves a place for us by His side. And all he asks for in return is that we love each other, pure and simple. Love without judgement, love without wanting anything else in return, love even when there is much to fear. When we face hatred with love, when we face fear with love, when we face evil with love, we bring into the world the light of God's love for all.

Look at all times to respond to fear, hatred and evil in your life with love. Will you be a witness to God's love for you, by sharing it with all those around you?

The right-hand side of the page is where you get to express yourself fully in a bullet journal format with space for 5 different elements.

The first box is titled **Reflection** and is your chance to write down your thoughts on the Scripture and, if you wish, to answer some of the questions that were posed. Alternatively, this is a great place to simply catch up with yourself and note where you currently are on your spiritual journey this week. *Note that at the end of the book I've added a few blank lined pages for any extra reflections or thoughts you wish to share.*

• WEEK OF:

Reflection

Thanks

Guidance

Prayers

Blessings

The next section is titled **Thanks** and this is an opportunity to thank God for everything you have in your life. What are you grateful for? Journal your gratitude here.

Next up is the section titled **Guidance**. What challenges face you this week? Share with God your worries and concerns. If you ask Him to teach and guide you, He will.

This guided prayer journal wouldn't be much use without the **Prayers** section! Write down your prayers for yourself and others as you move through the week.

And finally, we have a section for **Blessings**. Here you can write down any answered prayers, special surprises or well-earned achievements that come your way this week.

Of course, everything above are just my suggestions. This is your journal now and you should use it freely as you wish.

Enjoy your journey with God.

She is clothed with strength and dignity;
she can laugh at the days to come.
~ Proverbs 31:25

> *Therefore do not worry about tomorrow,*
> *for tomorrow will worry about itself.*
> *Each day has enough trouble of its own.*
> *~ Matthew 6:34*

Tomorrow Will Take Care of Itself

Regrets from the past and fears for the future, it's an all-too-common story. We all do it to a greater or lesser extent, we're only human. Only God is perfect and the good news is that He is with you always. So, don't let worry pile up on worry; most worries never even materialise. And when some of them do, we confront them and push through. We can do this because, as Matthew says, when we trust in God's will we need not worry about tomorrow because God will provide the answers.

*Is your life full of drama? Do you sometime make mountains out of molehills!? God wants you to calm down. This week, try to stay just in the present, what does God ask of you **today**. Tomorrow will take care of itself.*

1

• **WEEK OF:**

*Reflection*_____

_____

_____

_____

_____

_____

_____

*Thanks*_____

_____

_____

_____

_____

_____

*Guidance*_____

_____

_____

_____

_____

_____

*Prayers*_____

_____

_____

_____

_____

_____

*Blessings*_____

_____

_____

_____

_____

_____

> *Jesus told him,*
> *"Don't be afraid; just believe."*
> *- Mark 5:36*

Who's Looking After You?

Do you have children? Do you reassure them that everything is going to be okay? Often that's all that young children need to let go of their fears. If mummy says everything will be fine then that's good enough for them... they believe you. Let Jesus do the same for you. Trust in Him. Let God reassure you the same way you reassure your kids. Everything is going to be okay; just believe.

Do you take time to let God wrap His arms around you? What might that look like? Let God be a constant comfort in your life.

3

• **WEEK OF:**

Reflection_____

Thanks_____

Guidance_____

Prayers_____

Blessings_____

Look for the Helpers

Do you see God working in your life? In times of need do you see Him lending a helping hand? Just as God works through you, God works through other people too. When you are in need other people will come to your aid, both directly and indirectly. This is God. This is how He is with you... always.

Write down the times you were in need and you received help. Where did this help come from? Can you see where you were helped indirectly, perhaps by people you don't even know!?

• **WEEK OF:**

*Reflection*_____

_____

_____

_____

_____

_____

_____

*Thanks*_____

_____

_____

_____

_____

_____

_____

*Guidance*_____

_____

_____

_____

_____

_____

_____

*Prayers*_____

_____

_____

_____

_____

_____

_____

*Blessings*_____

_____

_____

_____

_____

_____

_____

> *Consider it pure joy, my brothers and sisters, whenever you face trials of many kinds because you know that the testing of your faith produces perseverance. Let perseverance finish its work so that you may be mature and complete, not lacking anything. - James 1:2-4*

Joy is Not Optional

The Bible demands that we be joyful. Joy is not optional; we must feel it! But how can we feel joyful when confronted with very real problems and suffering. The answer is in perseverance. When confronted with sorrow, when our faith is tested again and again, it is through perseverance that we can truly appreciate the joy that comes from faith. When we look back at our strength and determination to keep moving forward with God we will experience joy as we step with Him, back into the light.

How joyful would you be if you knew, for sure, that there was nothing, absolutely nothing in this world to worry about! Can you imagine the joy you would feel if you knew for sure, 100%, that you had a Father by your side to protect you at all times?

• **WEEK OF:**

*Reflection*_____
_____
_____
_____
_____
_____
_____

*Thanks*_____
_____
_____
_____
_____
_____
_____

*Guidance*_____
_____
_____
_____
_____
_____
_____

*Prayers*_____
_____
_____
_____
_____
_____
_____

*Blessings*_____
_____
_____
_____
_____
_____
_____

> *But when you ask, you must believe and not doubt, because the one who doubts is like a wave of the sea, blown and tossed by the wind. ~ James 1:6*

Don't Waste Time Doubting

God loves you, so believe it! Be bold and brave and share your thoughts and prayers with Him. Ask for His help and you will receive from Him all the guidance you could need... if you just believe. You don't need to trust in yourself or anybody else around you... just pause, take a breath and then ask with conviction. Share your concerns, worries and fears never doubting that He will answer you.

Do you sometimes doubt God's love? Do you worry that your prayers are too insignificant for Him to listen to? Could you try this week to cast aside your doubts and pray with conviction? What would that look like?

• **WEEK OF:**

*Reflection*_____
_____
_____
_____
_____
_____
_____
_____

*Thanks*_____
_____
_____
_____
_____
_____
_____
_____

*Guidance*_____
_____
_____
_____
_____
_____
_____
_____

*Prayers*_____
_____
_____
_____
_____
_____
_____

*Blessings*_____
_____
_____
_____
_____
_____
_____

> *Trust in the Lord with all your heart and lean not on your own understanding; in all your ways*
> *submit to him, and he will make your paths straight. - Proverbs 3:5-6*

Unmanageable Lives

It can be tempting to think that we humans, who have managed to shoot rockets into space and walk on the moon, can also know everything there is to know. And yet, many of the mysteries of life and death remain unknown; and much of what affects our every day is completely out of our individual control. So, knowing this, what can we do to get through all this chaos? We can trust in God's love for us, seek to practice His teachings in our daily life, and look to Him for guidance along our path.

Do you remember to pray when you feel the weight of earthly chaos all around you? Do you ask God to lift that load, and show you the way?

• **WEEK OF:**

*Reflection*_____
_____
_____
_____
_____
_____
_____

*Thanks*_____
_____
_____
_____
_____
_____
_____

*Guidance*_____
_____
_____
_____
_____
_____
_____

*Prayers*_____
_____
_____
_____
_____
_____
_____

*Blessings*_____
_____
_____
_____
_____
_____
_____

> *For you created my inmost being; you knit me together in my mother's womb. I praise you because I am fearfully and wonderfully made; your works are wonderful, I know that full well.*
> *~ Psalm 139:13-14*

Feel Unique

Each one of us is unique. There is no-one on this earth – populated with over seven billion people – who has the exact same combination of features, talents and skills, nor the exact same nose, or eyes or belly button! We are each of us God's creation, and each one of us is astonishingly complex, from our DNA to the depth of emotions in our soul. Each one of us is beautiful.

Know that God has made you unique, complex and beautiful. How will you use all that God has given you to carry out His will?

• **WEEK OF:**

Reflection_____
_____
_____
_____
_____
_____
_____

Thanks_____
_____
_____
_____
_____
_____
_____

Guidance_____
_____
_____
_____
_____
_____
_____

Prayers_____
_____
_____
_____
_____
_____
_____

Blessings_____
_____
_____
_____
_____
_____
_____

> *A friend loves at all times, and a brother is born for a time of adversity.*
> *~ Proverbs 17:17*

We Need One Another

No man (or woman) is an island. We are social animals and we need to stay connected to our fellows. For most of us that means our friends and family. Can we, do we, replicate the love God has for us with our friends and family? If not, why not? Maybe they don't reciprocate the love that we would freely give them. What then? God would have us carry his message of love into the world and we can always find ways to express that love if we look around us.

Do you have fellowship in your life? Are you a loving and giving member of your community? What are some ways that you can be available for others? Ask God for guidance.

• **WEEK OF:**

Reflection_____

_____

_____

_____

_____

_____

_____

Thanks_____

_____

_____

_____

_____

_____

Guidance_____

_____

_____

_____

_____

_____

Prayers_____

_____

_____

_____

_____

_____

Blessings_____

_____

_____

_____

_____

_____

> *The Lord is good to those whose hope is in him, to the one who seeks him; it is good to wait quietly for the salvation of the Lord. ~ Lamentations 3:25-26*

Patience is a Virtue

Modern life is very hectic and we don't often have the one quality we need most to get through it: patience! We are always so keen to get results, as soon as possible, immediately! But our relationship with God cannot be hurried. It takes a lifetime of learning, and so the first thing we must learn is to be patient. Just as Jesus hung on the cross patiently waiting for God's salvation, we too know that living faithfully and waiting patiently will bring us the answers we seek.

Take note of the times when you are most impatient; learn to breathe and wait for those moments to pass. Will you renew your hope in God today, by asking him to help you be patient?

• **WEEK OF:**

*Reflection*_____

_____

_____

_____

_____

_____

_____

*Thanks*_____

_____

_____

_____

_____

_____

*Guidance*_____

_____

_____

_____

_____

_____

*Prayers*_____

_____

_____

_____

_____

_____

*Blessings*_____

_____

_____

_____

_____

_____

> *So what shall I do?*
> *I will pray with my spirit, but I will also pray with my understanding; I will sing with my spirit, but I will also sing with my understanding.*
> *~ 1 Corinthians 14:15*

We Don't Have All the Answers

Life, especially these days, is full of uncertainty and we do not have all the answers. We cannot see into the future or fast-forward our lives like a movie to know how it ends. So we have to have faith that the decisions and choices we make are good, and we can only do that with the information we have. Thankfully, the Bible gives us all the guidance we need to make good choices in all of the most important areas of our lives.

It is normal to feel anxious when you don't have all the answers to the questions your day-to-day life poses. Will you place your trust in the Lord, and ask Him for guidance?

• **WEEK OF:**

*Reflection*_____
_____
_____
_____
_____
_____
_____

*Thanks*_____
_____
_____
_____
_____
_____
_____

*Guidance*_____
_____
_____
_____
_____
_____
_____

*Prayers*_____
_____
_____
_____
_____
_____
_____

*Blessings*_____
_____
_____
_____
_____
_____
_____

> *Teach me, and I will be quiet; show me where I have been wrong. How painful are honest words! ~ Job 6:24-25*

Be Honest with Yourself

Jesus is the ultimate teacher, and in his teachings we learn that we must repent of our sins to find eternal joy. God knows all of our sins and encourages us to ask for forgiveness. But it isn't always easy to admit when we are wrong; so, we need to take time every day and be big enough to look at the mistakes we have made, so that we can learn from them. For only by learning from our sins, will we know how to repent of them fully.

Take time every day to look honestly at yourself. Will you ask God for courage to admit your sins, and then ask for him to remove those sins from your soul?

• **WEEK OF:**

*Reflection*_____

_____

_____

_____

_____

_____

_____

*Thanks*_____

_____

_____

_____

_____

_____

_____

*Guidance*_____

_____

_____

_____

_____

_____

_____

*Prayers*_____

_____

_____

_____

_____

_____

_____

*Blessings*_____

_____

_____

_____

_____

_____

_____

> *Be strong and courageous. Do not be afraid or terrified because of them, for the Lord your God goes with you; he will never leave you nor forsake you. ~ Deuteronomy 31:6*

Take God with You

Marching into the unknown is scary, even terrifying at times. Can you remember a time that you were terrified? Sorrow is hard but terror is awful. Terror is fear out of control, terror is not good. When Moses told the Israelites to be strong and courageous, he was giving them good advice because the alternative was chaos. God goes with you, everywhere, so make use of Him. Get into the habit of trusting Him completely all the time. You'll be glad you did.

Do you have fair weather faith or do you have a faith that works under all circumstances? God is by your side, acknowledge Him daily.

• **WEEK OF:**

*Reflection*_____
_____
_____
_____
_____
_____
_____

*Thanks*_____
_____
_____
_____
_____
_____
_____

*Guidance*_____
_____
_____
_____
_____
_____
_____

*Prayers*_____
_____
_____
_____
_____
_____

*Blessings*_____
_____
_____
_____
_____
_____

... a time to weep and a time to laugh, a time to mourn and a time to dance ... He has made everything beautiful in its time. - Ecclesiastes 3:4-11

To Everything There is a Season

It's often only after you've been through a challenging time that you realize that you were strong enough. But during the darkest moments, it can seem that this is the time that you're finally going to break. But to every season there is a time, and we must stay faithful through every season, knowing that God is with us and that we are on His path. We cannot avoid the challenges that come our way, but we can get through them with God's grace.

Know that though you may weep today, tomorrow you will laugh. Will you make time today to commit your faith to God?

• **WEEK OF:**

Reflection_____

_____

_____

_____

_____

_____

_____

Thanks_____

_____

_____

_____

_____

_____

Guidance_____

_____

_____

_____

_____

_____

Prayers_____

_____

_____

_____

_____

_____

Blessings_____

_____

_____

_____

_____

_____

Carry each other's burdens, and in this way you will fulfill the law of Christ.
- Galatians 6:2

Be a Good Friend

You know you have a good friend if they are ready at any time with an open door and a cup of coffee ready to listen to any and all of your worries and concerns. Jesus asks us to be that good friend to all around us; be sure to take time out to check in with those around you, and simply listen. And in the middle of the night, when we are awake alone with our own thoughts, if we need someone to listen to us, then we know that God is always available!

The love of Christ is about caring for others whenever they are in need, even if all they need is someone to talk to. Do you take time to share the burdens of those around you?

• **WEEK OF:**

Reflection_____
_____
_____
_____
_____
_____

Thanks_____
_____
_____
_____
_____
_____

Guidance_____
_____
_____
_____
_____
_____

Prayers_____
_____
_____
_____
_____
_____

Blessings_____
_____
_____
_____
_____
_____

> *Peace I leave with you;*
> *my peace I give you. I do not give to you*
> *as the world gives. Do not let your*
> *hearts be troubled and do not be afraid.*
> *~ John 14:27*

Keep the Peace

Worries are contagious, like the common cold. You start the day feeling great but friends, family and colleagues bring their worries into your orbit and before long you're coming down with something! Time to follow Jesus. Pray for others and let your peace serve as an example. Take His peace, keep some for yourself and leave the rest with others.

Write down some of the ways you can help others, but also some of the ways you can't. Does worrying on behalf of others help them or you? What does peace look like in your life?

• **WEEK OF:**

*Reflection*_____
_____
_____
_____
_____
_____
_____

*Thanks*_____
_____
_____
_____
_____
_____
_____

*Guidance*_____
_____
_____
_____
_____
_____
_____

*Prayers*_____
_____
_____
_____
_____
_____
_____

*Blessings*_____
_____
_____
_____
_____
_____
_____

They will stumble over one another as though fleeing from the sword, even though no one is pursuing them.
~ Leviticus 26:37

Faith Vs Fear

The opposite of faith is fear and the opposite of strong faith is terror. When we fear, or fear too much, we have lost our faith and the results can be catastrophic. In fear, we can flee blindly even when nothing is pursuing us. This is when we turn to destructive temptations like drugs, alcohol, gambling or shopping as a way to numb away the pain we're feeling. Choosing love and faith over fear is hard, but choose it we must.

Write down the things that make you scared. Write down the ways you might run away from these fears. Sit with God, sit with your fears and wait for them to melt away. No one is pursuing you.

• **WEEK OF:**

Reflection_____

_____

_____

_____

_____

_____

Thanks_____

_____

_____

_____

_____

Guidance_____

_____

_____

_____

_____

Prayers_____

_____

_____

_____

_____

Blessings_____

_____

_____

_____

_____

> *Praise the Lord; Give thanks to the Lord, for he is good; his love endures forever. ~ Psalm 106:1*

Count Your Blessings

With a joyful heart, we count our blessings and give thanks. Even in the most challenging times, we can find gratitude for the very fact that we know God is with us and His love is never-ending. We are grateful that we wake every morning ready to deepen our commitment to God and to go forth in the world as a channel of His peace and love.

God is good, and loves you.
How will you go forth today to bring God's message of love to others?

• **WEEK OF:**

Reflection_____
_____
_____
_____
_____
_____
_____
_____

Thanks_____
_____
_____
_____
_____
_____
_____

Guidance_____
_____
_____
_____
_____
_____
_____

Prayers_____
_____
_____
_____
_____
_____
_____

Blessings_____
_____
_____
_____
_____
_____
_____

The wicked flee though no one pursues, but the righteous are as bold as a lion.
- Proverbs 28:1

Fear Nothing

We give glory to God who gives us strength and courage to be bold in the face of adversity! The Word of God gives us our purpose in life, and when we live our lives according to His commandments, we can stand up and declare that we fear nothing. We know that His never-ending love for us will lead us to a place of peace, tranquility and joy.

There are times when our faith is tested, but we remain strong in our commitment to the Lord. Do you remain faithful, so that you can face life's uncertainties as boldly as a lion?

• **WEEK OF:**

*Reflection*_____
_____
_____
_____
_____
_____
_____

*Thanks*_____
_____
_____
_____
_____
_____
_____

*Guidance*_____
_____
_____
_____
_____
_____
_____

*Prayers*_____
_____
_____
_____
_____
_____
_____

*Blessings*_____
_____
_____
_____
_____
_____
_____

Do not judge, and you will not be judged. Do not condemn, and you will not be condemned. Forgive, and you will be forgiven. ~ Luke 6:37

Be Slow to Judge

It seems that everywhere around us there are ways in which we are encouraged to judge each other and ourselves: social media, advertisements, reality programs that judge people's skill or talent. With all of that noise around us, it is hard not to fall into the trap of both disdain for others and self-pity for ourselves. But God sees us for what we are, and will always forgive even the greatest sinners; so, who then are we to judge?

You never know what other people are going through, so be slow to judge, and be kind to yourself too. Are you ready to forgive others and be forgiven?

• **WEEK OF:**

Reflection_____
_____
_____
_____
_____
_____
_____

Thanks_____
_____
_____
_____
_____
_____
_____

Guidance_____
_____
_____
_____
_____
_____
_____

Prayers_____
_____
_____
_____
_____
_____
_____

Blessings_____
_____
_____
_____
_____
_____
_____

Let us not become weary in doing good, for at the proper time we will reap a harvest if we do not give up.
~ Galatians 6:9

Helping Others

Love is as love does. We don't just pray for others, we actively go out and help them. No reward is greater than the sense of satisfaction we feel when we help others, asking for nothing in return. As God freely gives to you, give freely of yourself to others. We need not get overwhelmed by the suffering of others, rather we do what we can, one day at a time. When we help others we get out of ourselves and our own worries, we are free.

Is there a neighbor, friend or relative who needs your help today. What about a stranger? Where can you do the most good?

• **WEEK OF:**

Reflection_____
_____
_____
_____
_____
_____
_____

Thanks_____
_____
_____
_____
_____
_____
_____

Guidance_____
_____
_____
_____
_____
_____
_____

Prayers_____
_____
_____
_____
_____
_____
_____

Blessings_____
_____
_____
_____
_____
_____
_____

> *"Have faith in God," Jesus answered. "Truly I tell you, if anyone says to this mountain, 'Go, throw yourself into the sea,' and does not doubt in their heart but believes that what they say will happen, it will be done for them. Therefore I tell you, whatever you ask for in prayer, believe that you have received it, and it will be yours."*
> *~ Mark 11:22-24*

Whatever You Ask For

God has said that he will provide for us, and yet we continue to doubt. But a toddler who is learning to walk never doubts that their parent will be there to catch them if they fall. God says that we should be more like such trusting children. Believing with all our heart, persevering in our faith, that He will be there whenever we need Him most. Because He already is!

When you know God's presence in your life, then you can believe in Him with all your heart. How will you reaffirm your faith this week?

• **WEEK OF:**

*Reflection*_____
_____
_____
_____
_____
_____
_____

*Thanks*_____
_____
_____
_____
_____
_____

*Guidance*_____
_____
_____
_____
_____
_____

*Prayers*_____
_____
_____
_____
_____
_____

*Blessings*_____
_____
_____
_____
_____
_____

> *You will seek me and find me when you seek me with all your heart.*
> *~ Jeremiah 29:13*

Seek Him Out

Too often we expect that God should come to us – but in truth, God calls us to seek Him out. It is not enough to simply declare that you believe in God; nor is it enough to recite the same old prayers by rote, and then stand back waiting for Him to reveal his plans for you. Rather, He wants you to commit to a relationship with Him based on love and understanding; to seek Him out by actively engaging with Scripture; sharing with Him all that is in your heart.

It's important to make time for God in your life. What do you do every day to seek God in your life? Do you seek Him with all your heart?

• **WEEK OF:**

*Reflection*_____

_____

_____

_____

_____

_____

_____

*Thanks*_____

_____

_____

_____

_____

_____

*Guidance*_____

_____

_____

_____

_____

_____

*Prayers*_____

_____

_____

_____

_____

_____

*Blessings*_____

_____

_____

_____

_____

_____

> *The Lord is close to the brokenhearted and saves those who are crushed in spirit. ~ Psalm 34:18*

God Will See You Through

As human beings our spirits are fragile and prone to be broken repeatedly. No matter how tough we act we are not immune to crushing sadness and disappointment. We cannot avoid these obstacles indefinitely. The death of a loved one, the loss of a job, loss of earnings or separation from friends, these and many more traumas can arrive unannounced at any time and take the floor out from under us. Cry out to God for help in these times and He will comfort you, support you and, in time, heal you.

Can you look back at a sorrow and hardship and see that God was with you? How did God help you mend a broken heart? Who did He send to help you?

• **WEEK OF:**

Reflection_____
_____
_____
_____
_____
_____
_____
_____

Thanks_____
_____
_____
_____
_____
_____
_____

Guidance_____
_____
_____
_____
_____
_____
_____

Prayers_____
_____
_____
_____
_____
_____
_____

Blessings_____
_____
_____
_____
_____
_____
_____

> *"Martha, Martha," the Lord answered, "you are worried and upset about many things, but few things are needed — or indeed only one."*
> *- Luke 10:41-42*

The Bigger Picture

Our lives are so hectic these days, with the pressures of work and commitments; many of us are juggling a lot at once, and desperately willing for everything to go well. Sometimes we can get so caught up in the details, we forget to see the bigger picture. We can get caught in a loop of desperately seeking perfection in all areas of our lives. But the truth is that there is only one thing in our lives that will ever be perfect and that is the pure love that God has for us.

Will you choose to spend less time worrying about outward perfection, and focus more on your relationship with God, his love and the blessings He gives you?

• **WEEK OF:**

Reflection _____
_____
_____
_____
_____
_____
_____

Thanks _____
_____
_____
_____
_____
_____

Guidance _____
_____
_____
_____
_____
_____

Prayers _____
_____
_____
_____
_____
_____

Blessings _____
_____
_____
_____
_____
_____

> *No temptation has overtaken you except what is common to mankind.*
> *And God is faithful; he will not let you be tempted beyond what you can bear. But when you are tempted, he will also provide a way out so that you can endure it.*
> *~ 1 Corinthians 10:13*

Don't Give Up

They say, "There's nothing new under the sun". Whatever challenge or hardship you're going through right now, others have been through the same... and worse. Other women have trodden this path before you and you too will find your way through. And when you are tempted to cut corners, to find an easier or softer way, God will be there to help guide you back onto the right path. Don't give up, let Him take you by the hand.

Are you tempted to give up and sink into self-pity? Write down your temptations. Ask God to remove them or show you the way past them.

49

• **WEEK OF:**

Reflection_____
_____
_____
_____
_____
_____
_____

Thanks_____
_____
_____
_____
_____
_____

Guidance_____
_____
_____
_____
_____
_____

Prayers_____
_____
_____
_____
_____
_____

Blessings_____
_____
_____
_____
_____
_____

For I am convinced that neither death nor life, neither angels nor demons, neither the present nor the future, nor any powers, neither height nor depth, nor anything else in all creation, will be able to separate us from the love of God that is in Christ Jesus our Lord. ~ Romans 8:38-39

Unconditional Love

God loves us like we love our children, with unconditional love. They may behave badly and they might make bad choices, but we will continue to love them no matter what. And so it is with God's love for you. There's nothing you can do to separate yourself from God, even if you turn away from Him when you turn back, there He will be, patiently waiting. Nothing can change that.

If you feel guilty for anything, write it down. Offer it to God in your prayers, He will not turn away from you.

51

• **WEEK OF:**

*Reflection*_____

_____

_____

_____

_____

_____

_____

*Thanks*_____

_____

_____

_____

_____

_____

_____

*Guidance*_____

_____

_____

_____

_____

_____

_____

*Prayers*_____

_____

_____

_____

_____

_____

_____

*Blessings*_____

_____

_____

_____

_____

_____

The Lord is my light and my salvation—whom shall I fear? The Lord is the stronghold of my life—of whom shall I be afraid? ~ Psalm 27:1

Move into the Light

In the darkest of times, people still find the light they need to carry on. We know that light is the love of God, the courage and the hope He gives us. Even as we suffer through whatever is challenging us, we can look back at past challenges and see that we have got through them thanks to God's presence in our lives. This is our faith. We can go forward every day, knowing that He remains by our side and we do not need to fear.

List the times that has God been there for you in the past. Are you strong in your faith to entrust all future challenges in your life to Him?

• **WEEK OF:**

Reflection_____
_____
_____
_____
_____
_____
_____

Thanks_____
_____
_____
_____
_____
_____
_____

Guidance_____
_____
_____
_____
_____
_____
_____

Prayers_____
_____
_____
_____
_____
_____
_____

Blessings_____
_____
_____
_____
_____
_____
_____

> *He says,*
> *"Be still, and know that I am God."*
> *~ Psalm 46:10*

Take a Time Out

Life is busy: there are so many demands on us, and there never seems to be enough time to get everything done. And when we're not racing around getting things done, then we're chasing the many thoughts in our head as we plan and worry for the future! But God says that we must take time out from all of this, recognize His presence in our lives, and see that in Him we can find "our refuge and our strength" to help us through all things.

God is with you in every moment of the day. Are you taking time every day to feel God's presence in your life?

• **WEEK OF:**

*Reflection*_____
_____
_____
_____
_____
_____

*Thanks*_____
_____
_____
_____
_____
_____

*Guidance*_____
_____
_____
_____
_____
_____

*Prayers*_____
_____
_____
_____
_____

*Blessings*_____
_____
_____
_____
_____

> *So do not worry, saying, 'What shall we eat?' or 'What shall we drink?' or 'What shall we wear?' For the pagans run after all these things, and your heavenly Father knows that you need them. But seek first his kingdom and his righteousness, and all these things will be given to you as well.*
> *~ Matthew 6:31-33*

Want Vs Need

God knows what we need! Isn't that great news? We spend a lot of our lives chasing after material goods. Of course, we need the basics to survive, but if we look at ourselves honestly, we can see that so much of what we desire is just unnecessary stuff. When we focus more on the real things that matter – love for our neighbors, seeking humility, living in God's grace, then we begin to understand what is really valuable and worth chasing.

Make a list of all the things that you desire, cross off all the things that are not essential for your physical and spiritual well-being. Are you ready now to ask God to provide the things that really matter?

- **WEEK OF:**

Reflection_____

_____

_____

_____

_____

_____

_____

Thanks_____

_____

_____

_____

_____

_____

_____

Guidance_____

_____

_____

_____

_____

_____

_____

Prayers_____

_____

_____

_____

_____

_____

_____

Blessings_____

_____

_____

_____

_____

_____

Ask and it will be given to you; seek and you will find; knock and the door will be opened to you. ~ Luke 11:9

Remain Persistent in Prayer

My father had an expression "If you don't ask, you don't get!" and that can be applied to our prayer life too! Ask God for help, ask Him for yourself and ask Him for others, ask Him for anything. God may say "no" or He may say "wait", but He will give you an answer. Remain persistent in prayer and trust that God will answer you.

This week go into prayer overdrive. Supersize your prayers, be bold and hold nothing back!

• **WEEK OF:**

*Reflection*_____

_____

_____

_____

_____

_____

_____

*Thanks*_____

_____

_____

_____

_____

_____

*Guidance*_____

_____

_____

_____

_____

_____

*Prayers*_____

_____

_____

_____

_____

_____

*Blessings*_____

_____

_____

_____

_____

_____

> *Do not say, "Why were the old days better than these?" For it is not wise to ask such questions. ~ Ecclesiastes 7:10*

Trust God, Not Your Memory

Do not trust your memory! Have you noticed how quick our minds are to forget the challenges of our youth? There was a time when breaking up with a boyfriend meant the end of the world! The past wasn't better, the past was different. We could perhaps give ourselves some credit for the challenges we overcame in the past rather than wishing we were back there. And if the present seems uncomfortably daunting, we might trust that God will help us just like He did in the past.

*Maybe take a trip down memory lane this week with childhood friends or family. What were the old day **really** like? Take the time to celebrate your past victories and give thanks for the hardships overcome.*

• **WEEK OF:**

*Reflection*_____

*Thanks*_____

*Guidance*_____

*Prayers*_____

*Blessings*_____

> *... David triumphed over the Philistine with a sling and a stone; without a sword in his hand he struck down the Philistine and killed him.*
> *~ 1 Samuel 17:50*

Work With What You Have

When we're faced with new situations, and especially ones that are out of our immediate control, it's easy to fear that we are completely unprepared and not ready. We might try to gather as many tools as possible to face down whatever "giant" is ahead of us; but in the end you can only do your best with the tools you have. Just like David, we must trust that God will provide us with all we need to fight the battles ahead.

It is human nature to feel inadequate and to worry. Will you give those worries to God and ask him to give you the tools you need to vanquish your fears?

• **WEEK OF:**

Reflection_____

Thanks_____

Guidance_____

Prayers_____

Blessings_____

In Good Times and Bad, Stay Close to God

When things are going well, do you forget to seek God? It's easy enough to do. We might remember to thank God in our prayers or write in our gratitude journals, but do we really *look to the Lord and his strength* on a daily basis when everything's going our way. Or do we take back our will and congratulate ourselves on a life well lived? In good times and bad, stay close to God. Acknowledge His power and turn your will and your life over to Him, again and again.

A daily gratitude list is a great way to remind yourself daily of the blessings He bestows. Write down the ways in which God helped you this week.

• **WEEK OF:**

Reflection_____
_____
_____
_____
_____
_____
_____

Thanks_____
_____
_____
_____
_____
_____
_____

Guidance_____
_____
_____
_____
_____
_____
_____

Prayers_____
_____
_____
_____
_____
_____
_____

Blessings_____
_____
_____
_____
_____
_____

> *She is clothed with strength and dignity; she can laugh at the days to come. ~ Proverbs 31:25*

Laugh at the Unknown

Well now, this is a Scripture we can aspire to. The question is... how do we get there? Make a decision to turn your will and your life over to the care of God. Love, worship and obey God and He will give you the strength and the dignity you search for. And once you've given yourself to God completely, it is easy, or easier, to laugh at the days to come.

Do you pick and chose which parts of yourself you will give to God and which parts you will hold back for yourself? Perhaps try giving Him everything for a week. Write down what you might do differently?

• **WEEK OF:**

Reflection_____
_____
_____
_____
_____
_____
_____

Thanks_____
_____
_____
_____
_____
_____

Guidance_____
_____
_____
_____
_____
_____

Prayers_____
_____
_____
_____
_____

Blessings_____
_____
_____
_____
_____

> *Humble yourselves, therefore, under God's mighty hand, that he may lift you up in due time. Cast all your anxiety on him because he cares for you.*
> *~ 1 Peter 5:6-7*

Humility Equals Grace

Sometimes we have to make the somewhat uncomfortable choice... do we want to be right or do we want to be happy!? As the Pastor Rick Warren said, "Humility is not thinking less of yourself, but thinking of yourself less". When society is divided and at war with itself, we can choose whether to fight or surrender. Sometimes it pays to keep quiet, to admit we don't necessarily have all the answers. We can, with grace and humility, cast our anxieties on God and wait for Him to lift us up in due course.

Can we admit to our shortcomings? Can we also trust that we are doing the best we can under difficult circumstances? And can we trust that God will take up the slack?

• **WEEK OF:**

Reflection _____
_____
_____
_____
_____
_____
_____

Thanks _____
_____
_____
_____
_____
_____

Guidance _____
_____
_____
_____
_____
_____

Prayers _____
_____
_____
_____
_____
_____

Blessings _____
_____
_____
_____
_____
_____

Jesus immediately said to them :
"Take courage! It is I.
Don't be afraid."
~ Matthew 14:27

Take Courage

Faith takes courage. God will help us and guide us but only if we embrace him with our unwavering faith. Fear is the flipside of faith and when fear comes, and it will, we must embrace God with our faith anew and with as much courage and bravery as we are able. God helps those who help themselves. What does that mean? In its simplest terms it means God will always help us if we choose to follow Him.

How courageous do you feel in the face of adversity? What do you need from God to feel more courageous? Ask Him in your prayers.

• **WEEK OF:**

*Reflection*_____
_____
_____
_____
_____
_____
_____

*Thanks*_____
_____
_____
_____
_____
_____
_____

*Guidance*_____
_____
_____
_____
_____
_____
_____

*Prayers*_____
_____
_____
_____
_____
_____
_____

*Blessings*_____
_____
_____
_____
_____
_____

Finally, brothers and sisters, whatever is true, whatever is noble, whatever is right, whatever is pure, whatever is lovely, whatever is admirable — if anything is excellent or praiseworthy — think about such things. ~ Philippians 4:8

Focus on the Positive

What a beautiful Scripture! If only the world was a reflection of these words. Instead, we are bombarded everyday with the opposite. Open the paper or turn on the TV and news of suffering, injustice, lies and violence come spilling out. No wonder we sometimes feel gloomy. But we have a choice. In our prayers we ask God to help those who we cannot help directly. Then we can turn our attention closer to home. God is good and His world is beautiful, if we know where to look. Let's think about that!

How much time do you spend absorbed in the ugly and unpleasant aspects of this world? What can we do this week to celebrate God's love? How can we bring truth, nobility and whatever is right into our lives and the lives of our neighbors today?

• **WEEK OF:**

Reflection_____

_____

_____

_____

_____

_____

_____

Thanks_____

_____

_____

_____

_____

_____

_____

Guidance_____

_____

_____

_____

_____

_____

_____

Prayers_____

_____

_____

_____

_____

_____

_____

Blessings_____

_____

_____

_____

_____

_____

_____

> *Do not be anxious about anything, but in every situation, by prayer and petition, with thanksgiving, present your requests to God.*
> *- Philippians 4:6*

Self-forgetting

Worry and anxiety blossom when they get stuck inside our own heads. That's why prayer is such a great antidote to worry. Instead of letting anxiety spin around wildly inside your mind, place it in a prayer and send it out to God. He loves to receive your worries. Once you have sent Him your prayers turn immediately to something outside yourself. Who can we help or comfort? As it says in the Saint Francis Prayer, it is better... "To love, than to be loved. For it is by self-forgetting that one finds."

Write down your worries and take them to God. Now who do you know who also has worries? Give them a call this week.

• **WEEK OF:**

Reflection_____
_____
_____
_____
_____
_____
_____

Thanks_____
_____
_____
_____
_____
_____
_____

Guidance_____
_____
_____
_____
_____
_____
_____

Prayers_____
_____
_____
_____
_____
_____

Blessings_____
_____
_____
_____
_____
_____

So do not fear, for I am with you; do not be dismayed, for I am your God. I will strengthen you and help you; I will uphold you with my righteous right hand. All who rage against you will surely be ashamed and disgraced; those who oppose you will be as nothing and perish. ~ Isaiah 41:10-11

Hand It Over

When we trust and know God as an ever-present force in our lives, then we know that we have no reason to fear whatever comes our way. We know that if we believe in our Lord as our Savior, that we can rely on him for our strength and our salvation.

List all your fears and worries and give them over to God. He is there to show you the way. Will you allow God to be the constant force in your life, that you can rely on no matter what?

• **WEEK OF:**

Reflection_____

_____

_____

_____

_____

_____

_____

Thanks_____

_____

_____

_____

_____

_____

Guidance_____

_____

_____

_____

_____

_____

Prayers_____

_____

_____

_____

_____

_____

Blessings_____

_____

_____

_____

_____

_____

Whether you turn to the right or to the left, your ears will hear a voice behind you, saying, "This is the way; walk in it."
- Isaiah 30:21

Your Better Angels

In the Bible we read how God sent angels, burning bushes, prophets and then Jesus himself to speak to His people and show them the way. Today we have bible study groups and pastors to help us understand the Word. Hearing His voice is not always that easy, and yet messages do come to us in myriad ways. When we pray for His guidance and take time to truly reflect, aligning our choices with God's teaching, then we will hear those words and know that we are on the correct path.

Consider the times when you've had to make difficult decisions. Did you look to God for guidance? Did you ask Him to show you the way?

• **WEEK OF:**

*Reflection*_____

_____
_____
_____
_____
_____
_____

*Thanks*_____

_____
_____
_____
_____
_____
_____

*Guidance*_____

_____
_____
_____
_____
_____
_____

*Prayers*_____

_____
_____
_____
_____
_____

*Blessings*_____

_____
_____
_____
_____
_____

> *Many are the plans in a person's heart,*
> *but it is the Lord's purpose that prevails.*
> *~ Proverbs 19:21*

God Has a Plan

Even when our personal plans don't go to plan, God's plan is at work! This may seem frustrating when we have been let down, or broken hearted, or when any number of circumstances cause our plans to fail. But God's plan for us is not that we avoid failure altogether, but that those failures can be part of a bigger picture. As we seek to deepen our trust in God, know that His purpose will be revealed.

List the times that your plans have gone awry, and what you learned from those experiences. Are you able to see when those experiences brought you closer to God?

• **WEEK OF:**

*Reflection*_____

_____

_____

_____

_____

_____

_____

*Thanks*_____

_____

_____

_____

_____

_____

_____

*Guidance*_____

_____

_____

_____

_____

_____

_____

*Prayers*_____

_____

_____

_____

_____

_____

_____

*Blessings*_____

_____

_____

_____

_____

_____

> *Dear children, let us not love with words or speech but with actions and in truth.*
> *- 1 John 3:18*

Acts of Kindness

We all know the saying, "Actions speak louder than words" and we all know that to be true. An act of kindness – even as simple as someone holding a door open for you – lets you know that someone has seen you, someone has taken a moment to care for you in some way. Even that smallest act is an expression of love, and is what God asks us to do.

We should all strive to be the person that cares. What ways can you demonstrate the love and truth of the Lord in acts of kindness or otherwise?

• **WEEK OF:**

*Reflection*_____
_____
_____
_____
_____
_____
_____

*Thanks*_____
_____
_____
_____
_____
_____

*Guidance*_____
_____
_____
_____
_____
_____

*Prayers*_____
_____
_____
_____
_____
_____

*Blessings*_____
_____
_____
_____
_____
_____

> *Your beauty should not come from outward adornment, such as elaborate hairstyles and the wearing of gold jewelry or fine clothes. Rather, it should be that of your inner self, the unfading beauty of a gentle and quiet spirit, which is of great worth in God's sight. ~ 1 Peter 3:3-4*

The Beauty Within

As women we feel a particular pressure from society to look good at all times, wear the right outfits, and to live up to impossible standards that only photoshopping can achieve! For some women, even the simple act of letting their hair turn gray naturally, is an act of defiance against the societal norms! But when we live righteously, we know that our true worth is not in our outward appearance, and that God cares not one bit for our new haircut, but for the beauty of our soul.

Are you able to see that your worth is not in your choice of outfit, but in your choice to follow the path that God has set you?

• **WEEK OF:**

*Reflection*_____

_____
_____
_____
_____
_____
_____

*Thanks*_____

_____
_____
_____
_____
_____
_____

*Guidance*_____

_____
_____
_____
_____
_____
_____

*Prayers*_____

_____
_____
_____
_____
_____
_____

*Blessings*_____

_____
_____
_____
_____
_____

> *Anxiety weighs down the heart,*
> *but a kind word cheers it up.*
> *~ Proverbs 12:25*

Have You Heard the Good News?

Those who have deep anxiety disorders know that often words are not enough, and we are all very thankful that there are therapies and support groups on hand for the most troubling mental health problems. But when we get caught up in the everyday worries, especially when we worry about things that are completely out of our control, then we know that having a friendly ear to listen can really help. The Word of God is also the cheerful news we need when we are troubled.

Turn to Scripture whenever you need a reminder that God loves you and that you are never alone. Will you share your worries with God today, and let Him be the friendly ear you need?

• **WEEK OF:**

Reflection_____
_____
_____
_____
_____
_____
_____

Thanks_____
_____
_____
_____
_____
_____
_____

Guidance_____
_____
_____
_____
_____
_____
_____

Prayers_____
_____
_____
_____
_____
_____
_____

Blessings_____
_____
_____
_____
_____
_____

> *Be completely humble and gentle;*
> *be patient, bearing with one*
> *another in love.*
> *~ Ephesians 4:2*

Pride Comes Before a Fall

Humble, gentle and patient? Completely? Easier said than done! The world moves so fast and other people can be so abrasive and mean, we feel like we have to fight for everything. In this dog-eat-dog world this Scripture feels like a tall order. Resentments and rationalizations stand between us and peace. Ask God for forgiveness in all situations. The sooner you can let go of pride the sooner you will find peace.

What are the benefits of keeping your cool? What are the benefits of losing your temper? What do you lose when forgiving someone and what do you gain?

• **WEEK OF:**

Reflection _____

Thanks _____

Guidance _____

Prayers _____

Blessings _____

> *But Moses said to God, "Who am I that I should go to Pharaoh and bring the Israelites out of Egypt?"*
> *And God said, "I will be with you..."*
> *~ Exodus 3:11-12*

Who am I?

Moses went to Pharaoh and asked him to free the Israelites. That took courage, more courage than Moses really possessed probably. But God told Moses that He would be with Him and that was enough for Moses. That should be enough for you too. God is with you whenever you have to tackle something that daunts you. Go forward with a good heart and a clear conscience and you have nothing to fear, God will take care of the rest.

Is there anything that you've been putting off? Make a list. See how many things you can tick off your list. Take God with you.

• **WEEK OF:**

*Reflection*_____

*Thanks*_____

*Guidance*_____

*Prayers*_____

*Blessings*_____

> *Let us then approach God's throne of grace with confidence, so that we may receive mercy and find grace to help us in our time of need. ~ Hebrews 4:16*

Ask for Help

Sometimes it is not easy to accept that we need help. We live in a world where we've been conditioned to think that, as long as we strive hard enough, we can achieve anything we want, on our own terms. So, when we come up against trouble, we might feel foolish or belittled to ask for help. And yet, God was willing to give the ultimate sacrifice – His only son – to help save us all from eternal damnation! There lies God's grace: despite our own arrogance, He still offers us help whenever we need it.

Have there been times when you've struggled to admit you need help? Are you willing to accept God's grace and ask Him for help?

93

• **WEEK OF:**

Reflection_____
_____
_____
_____
_____
_____

Thanks_____
_____
_____
_____
_____
_____

Guidance_____
_____
_____
_____
_____
_____

Prayers_____
_____
_____
_____
_____
_____

Blessings_____
_____
_____
_____
_____
_____

> *My command is this :*
> *Love each other as I have loved you.*
> *~ John 15:12*

Love Each Other

God's love for us is unconditional and boundless; it is through His love for us that He forgives our sins and reserves a place for us by His side. And all He asks for in return is that we love each other, pure and simple. Love without judgement, love without wanting anything else in return, love even when there is much to fear. When we face hatred with love, when we face fear with love, when we face evil with love, we bring into the world the light of God's love for all.

Try at all times to respond to fear, hatred and evil in your life with love. Will you be a witness to God's love for you, by sharing it with all those around you?

95

• **WEEK OF:**

*Reflection*_____

_____

_____

_____

_____

_____

_____

*Thanks*_____

_____

_____

_____

_____

_____

_____

*Guidance*_____

_____

_____

_____

_____

_____

_____

*Prayers*_____

_____

_____

_____

_____

_____

_____

*Blessings*_____

_____

_____

_____

_____

_____

_____

For I know that good itself does not dwell in me, that is, in my sinful nature. For I have the desire to do what is good, but I cannot carry it out. ~ Romans 7:18

Only God is Perfect

Do you ever promise yourself that you're going to behave a certain way, keep your cool, be loving and kind, be considerate of others... and then find yourself doing the complete opposite!? If the answer is yes, you're not alone... far from it. Only God is perfect. For us mortals there's acceptance, perseverance and patience... and that's with ourselves as well as others. You have your faults and you have your sins, don't beat yourself up for them. Take them to God everyday in your prayers and He will remove them, one day at a time.

Let God remove your faults and flaws. Identify the most uncomfortable aspects of your behavior and ask God, humbly but with conviction, to remove them. Ask willingly every day and leave the rest up to Him.

• **WEEK OF:**

Reflection_____
_____
_____
_____
_____
_____
_____

Thanks_____

_____

_____

_____

_____

_____

Guidance_____

_____

_____

_____

_____

_____

Prayers_____

_____

_____

_____

_____

_____

Blessings_____

_____

_____

_____

_____

_____

> *Those who know your name trust in you, for you, Lord, have never forsaken those who seek you.*
> *~ Psalm 9:10*

No Strings Attached

We sometimes fall into the trap of setting out conditions for our faith; we promise to follow God's Word, so long as he does x, y or z. But when we try to bargain with God, then we are not trusting His presence in our lives. Accepting this kind of unconditional trust is difficult, especially when we are faced with great challenges. But having faith in God does not mean that we will avoid challenging times, it means that He will be with us to help us through.

Are there times when you try to bargain with God? Trust in the Lord and He will not forsake you.

• **WEEK OF:**

Reflection_____

_____

_____

_____

_____

_____

_____

Thanks_____

_____

_____

_____

_____

_____

Guidance_____

_____

_____

_____

_____

_____

Prayers_____

_____

_____

_____

_____

_____

Blessings_____

_____

_____

_____

_____

_____

> *I know what it is to be in need, and I know what it is to have plenty. I have learned the secret of being content in any and every situation, whether well fed or hungry, whether living in plenty or in want. I can do all this through him who gives me strength. ~ Philippians 4:12-13*

Gratitude as a Habit

Gratitude, gratitude and more gratitude… you can never have enough of it! It is very hard, if not impossible, to be unhappy at the same time as being grateful. So, practising gratitude is one of the most important habits we can have. And as this Scripture tells us, it's not just being grateful for what we have, it's about living in want and *still* being grateful! God won't always give us what we want, but He will *always* give us what we need if we trust in Him. And for that we can be grateful.

When do you feel ungrateful and what you can do to turn that around? What are the most important things in your life that you can be grateful for, every single day?

• **WEEK OF:**

Reflection_____

Thanks_____

Guidance_____

Prayers_____

Blessings_____

You are the light of the world. A town built on a hill cannot be hidden. Neither do people light a lamp and put it under a bowl. Instead, they put it on its stand, and it gives light to everyone in the house. In the same way, let your light shine before others, that they may see your good deeds and glorify your Father in heaven. ~ Matthew 5:14-16

A Beacon of His Love

As women of faith we have one clear purpose: to do God's will and be a shining beacon of His love. We do not need to be big celebrities or have a captive audience to do this. We can shine our light even in the most mundane of situations: we can be a good neighbor, be an attentive friend, care for our families, conduct our business affairs with honesty and humility. We can share other's joy, be there for them when they suffer, and show through our actions and words what it means to live in God's love.

Even the smallest candle shines a light. What can you do this week to let your light shine?

• **WEEK OF:**

Reflection_____
_____
_____
_____
_____
_____
_____

Thanks_____
_____
_____
_____
_____
_____
_____

Guidance_____
_____
_____
_____
_____
_____
_____

Prayers_____
_____
_____
_____
_____
_____
_____

Blessings_____
_____
_____
_____
_____
_____

Thank you!

This journal is published by Kalogria Press, an independent publishing house run by husband-and-wife team, Grace and Jamie Sandford.

Kalogria Press focuses on providing Christian devotionals, guided journals and prayer books that speak to our experiences on our journey through faith. We hope that this journal has brought you closer to God.

If there is anything we could change or add to make this book more useful to you please get in touch at kalogriapress@gmail.com and help us to improve future editions.

Continue your journey with God at **www.kalogriapress.com**

Finally, if you have enjoyed this book please support us by leaving a review. Here is a direct link to the review page on Amazon:

www.kalogriapress.com/pray

Thank you and God bless

Also by Kalogria Press

www.kalogriapress.com/seeking-serenity

In these complicated times, where many aspects of our lives – our health, our families, our communities, our jobs – seem to be in jeopardy, it's easy to feel overwhelmed by uncertainty and fear.

By exploring how the Scriptures have enabled her to find peace when confronted with tragedy and uncertainty in her own life, Grace Sandford offers you this devotional and guided journal. Week by week, this journal will help you face your fears, bring them to God and find the serenity in faith to live an anxiety free life!

www.kalogriapress.com/relentless

Does it feel like a Christian woman's work is never done!? If your life feels #relentless then this is the Christian woman's devotional journal for you. Keep everything on track and remain relentlessly committed to Christ!

This 3-in-1 diary works as a prayer journal, daily devotional **and** weekly planner for the busy Christian mom, wife or single woman. Covering 52 weeks, with plenty of room to journal your prayers, give thanks and reflect with a devotional scripture verse, and a seven-day planner page to jot down your most important appointments and things to do.

Made in United States
Orlando, FL
24 April 2023

32427697R00072